SOUTH SEAS SAILOR

The Story of John Williams and his Ships

by

CECIL NORTHCOTT

GW00600653

LUTTERWORTH PRESS
GUILDFORD AND LONDON

First paperback edition 1980

ISBN 0 7188 2488 1

Copyright © 1965 Cecil Northcott

PRINTED PHOTOLITHO IN GREAT BRITAIN
BY EBENEZER BAYLIS AND SON, LTD.
THE TRINITY PRESS, WORCESTER, AND LONDON

CONTENTS

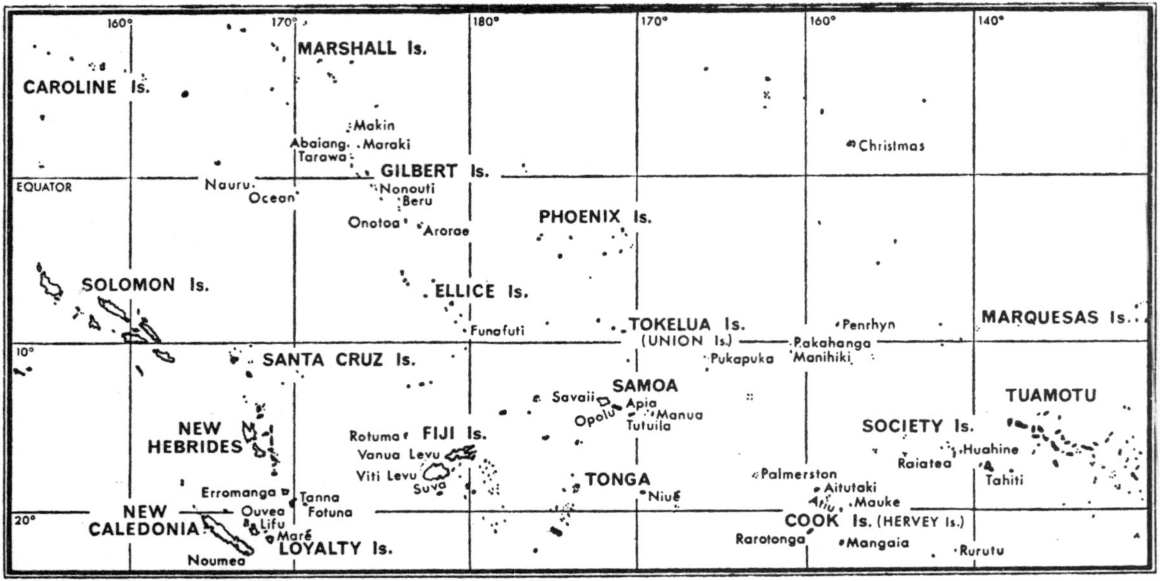
160°
170°
180°
170°
160°
140°
MARSHALL Is.
CAROLINE Is.
Makin
Abaiang
Maraki
Tarawa
Christmas
GILBERT Is.
EQUATOR
Nauru
Ocean
Nonouti
Beru
PHOENIX Is.
Onotoa
Arorae
SOLOMON Is.
ELLICE Is.
Funafuti
TOKELUA Is.
(UNION Is.)
Penrhyn
Pakahanga
Manihiki
MARQUESAS Is.
10°
SANTA CRUZ Is.
Pukapuka
SAMOA
Savaii
Apia
Opolu
Manua
Tutuila
TUAMOTU
NEW HEBRIDES
Rotuma
FIJI Is.
Vanua Levu
Viti Levu
Suva
SOCIETY Is.
Huahine
Raiatea
Tahiti
TONGA
Niue
Palmerston
Aitutaki
Atiu
Mauke
Erromanga
Tanna
Fotuna
Ouvea
Lifu
Maré
20°
NEW CALEDONIA
LOYALTY Is.
Noumea
COOK Is. (HERVEY Is.)
Rarotonga
Mangaia
Rurutu

I

LONDON BOY

WHEN he was fourteen the question arose in the family, "What is to be done with John?" He showed no special bent, but being such a "handy lad" a practical trade of some sort was clearly the best thing. There were few openings for apprentices in Tottenham or Edmonton, so the Williams family moved into London to Spencer Street, off the Goswell Road. It was a small brick house, basemented, in a long terrace, such as were then being built in hundreds on the northern flanks of London.

For John Williams the move meant a start in the world. On March 27, 1810, at the age of fourteen, he was indentured for seven years as an apprentice to Mr. Enoch Tonkin, a furnishing ironmonger, at 12, City Road. He started behind the counter weighing nails and learning the lengths of rods, the sizes of screws, and the uses of domestic fittings. He put on the black apron of the apprentice, and, like all apprentices of the day, "lived with the family". He had the shutters down and the shop open by seven each morning. City Road was then a residential neighbourhood, and Mr. Tonkin had a good business in supplying the houses with oil and household hardware. One day there was an urgent call for a bell to be hung in a customer's house and there was no workman available. John went and did the job well.

He also began, very early in his apprenticeship, wandering into the workshop which adjoined the shop. He watched a metal worker beat out a hinge, and another make a steel fender for a fireplace. One day, in the men's dinner hour, he tried his hand at using a big hammer and in manipulating a piece of white-hot iron from the blacksmith's forge. The handling of tools came naturally to him, and although he was there to learn the commercial side of the business only, Mr. Tonkin quickly saw that John was an all-round apprentice.

On Sundays he went home to Spencer Street and worshipped with his mother at Whitefield Tabernacle, Finsbury, where Mathew Wilks was minister. But she noticed that he sometimes "went unwillingly". One Sunday he was invited by some City Road apprentices to a local tavern which had a garden attached. He liked the jovial company and often made excuses to his mother so that he might join his friends there. But out of respect for her he still kept up chapel attendances, and on her part the prayers were more fervent that "the turning of his heart towards God" would soon come. "My course," said Williams in after years, "though not outwardly immoral was very wicked. I was regardless of the Holy Sabbath and a lover of pleasure more than a lover of God." But he neglected nothing in his work and gradually became in his spare time a first-class mechanic, at home at the anvil and the bench.

Then came "the turning point". He was eighteen years old when one Sunday he had arranged to spend the evening with his friends at the tavern. It was January 30, 1814, a date which Williams carefully recorded and always remembered. The young men he was to meet were late in turning up and Williams walked up and down the street impatiently. He waited under a street lamp and while there was seen by Mrs. Tonkin, his master's wife, on her way to the Tabernacle for the evening service. Knowing how worried his mother was about his "Sabbath breaking", Mrs. Tonkin began her gentle attack.

"Come with me, John, tonight to the Tabernacle."

"No," he replied, rather awkwardly, "I'll wait for them."

"But they may not come," she urged. "Come with me tonight. Mr. East of Birmingham is the special preacher tonight."

Standing under the flickering oil lamp in the City Road the older woman gradually persuaded the boy to go with her. It was a victory for persuasion and importunity. They went down the City Road to Finsbury Tabernacle, he feeling a little sheepish and she quietly elated at her small victory. That night the Rev. Timothy East preached from the text: "What is a man profited if he shall gain the whole world and lose his own soul? Or what shall a man give in exchange for his soul?"

It was a word straight to the point for the London boy, and in the quietness of his own heart as he sat next to Mrs. Tonkin, the act of conversion took place. "What is a man profited . . .?" That phrase rang in his ears and John Williams took his stand "among those who are on the Lord's side".

John Williams was now within twelve months of completing his indenture. He had been so useful to Mr. Tonkin that the shop and establishment in City Road were often left in his charge, for he was as capable at the forge and bench as behind the counter. But the "turning point" which had taken place during the sermon of Timothy East was a life direction. In the autumn of 1815 the annual missionary meetings of the Tabernacle Auxiliary of the London Missionary Society were held with more than usual enthusiasm. The news from the South Seas of heroic missionaries fired the eloquence of

10

the Tabernacle minister, Mathew Wilks. Williams was stirred, and "My heart," he says, "was frequently with the poor heathen." The desire to do something remained, but he did not act impulsively but gave time for the enthusiasm of the meetings to subside. For several months he kept the secret and then at last talked to Wilks about it. Wilks at once saw the simplicity of Williams's character and the deep surrender which lay in his offer to take the Gospel to the South Seas.

So in July, 1816, John Williams offered his services to the London Missionary Society.

The work called and Williams was ready to go. Mr. Tonkin released him from the seven months which remained of his apprenticeship, and on September 30, 1816, he, with eight other young missionaries, was ordained and farewelled before a congregation which thronged the Surrey Chapel.

A few weeks later John Williams was married to Mary Chauner. He was twenty and she nineteen. A month afterwards the ship *Harriet* fluttered down the Thames on a grey November afternoon carrying a pair of young hearts eagerly hoping.

2

OFF TO THE SOUTH SEAS

THE *HARRIET* made fast sailing to the coast of South America, and on December 29 entered the majestic harbour of Rio de Janeiro, while a prayer meeting was held on board to give thanks for the wonderful passage of six thousand miles in five weeks. The loveliness of Rio, the harbour studded with islands and the flower-covered mountains looking down on a blue sea filled John and Mary Williams with delight. The young Londoners, freed from the confined shop and foggy streets of their city, revelled in the beautiful town and the harbour's matchless beauty.

At Rio the Williams's were joined by four more missionaries and the party set out again in the *Harriet* for the stormy passage of Cape Horn and across the Pacific to Tasmania and northward to Sydney, where they arrived six months from home. It took them another six months to reach Tahiti, being delayed by a storm off New Zealand, during which they were driven three hundred miles out of their course.

But at last the long voyage was over and, on

November 16, 1817, the party of missionaries saw the tall peaks of Tahiti stand above the horizon and, as they looked on the white beaches lapped by the blue sea, their hearts "leaped for joy at the sight of the long-watched-for land". They were carried shoulder-high through the waves to the Mission House which had been built nearly thirty years before for Captain Bligh of the *Bounty*. A warm Pacific wind fanned Williams's cheek as he stood in stiff broadcloth looking out from the mission compound over the scene of waving palms and breaking surf. He was in the world of which he had dreamed and there, looking in at the compound gate, was a laughing group of the Tahitians he had come to serve.

When Williams crossed, the day after his arrival, to the island of Eimeo, the headquarters of the Mission, he saw the great chapel which King Pomare had erected with its 133 windows, 29 doors, 3 pulpits and 280 pillars, looking, in Williams's words, "like a hay-stack".

He also noticed on the beach at Eimeo a half-finished, large sailing boat which the missionaries had given up as too big a job to complete. They had started it partly as a present to the king, who wished to start trading, and partly as a "gospel-ship" to visit other islands. It was a chance for Williams to show his skill. The keel was already laid and the ribs ready for planking, so Williams bustled round and within eight days had finished the ship. In a smith's apron he stood in front of an open-air forge and made the bolts and iron bands for the sides. The rest sawed and planed and finished off the decking. Williams was on board the *Harriet* which helped the amateur shipwrights.

But there were many doubts about the launch. Pomare had already condemned the ship as ill-fated but was persuaded to come to the launching. Crowds of people from all over the island poured down to the beach to see the sight. Ropes were passed over the stern and a hundred pairs of hands caught them on both sides. Standing at the bows Pomare hurled a bottle of wine at the bows, and at the crashing noise of glass the men on his side were frightened and dropped the ropes, but on the other side the men pulled and the ship heeled over on to the beach. The cry went up, "Alas, the poor ship," and the king went off in disgust.

Stripping off their coats the missionaries raised her on to an even keel and got her back on to the stocks. It was a tough job, with many doubtful spectators looking on. Two days later the launch was again attempted and the same preparations were made and the two hundred men held the ropes. But standing in front of them, so that he could be seen by all the pullers, was an old man who shouted and exhorted to "put fire into the men". It was his professional job on the eve of battle, and, fired by his oratory, the two hundred men strained at the ropes. She moved, and slid gracefully into the lagoon. It added not a little to Williams's prestige. Besides, he now had a ship to visit the other islands.

His chance came when two chiefs from Huahine, away to the windward of Eimeo, arrived asking for teachers. The fame of the new religion often spread in this way in the South Seas. These two chiefs had come to see the new missionaries at work. To Williams it appeared an ideal chance to visit Huahine. So the little party set out in the home-made ship, the Williams's with their six-months-old baby. They were two days in the open sea between the islands, Williams standing in the prow with the chiefs looking eagerly for the mountain tops of the island. Along the beach a friendly crowd of people cheered them on landing, especially when they knew whom the chiefs had brought back. The baby was lifted from hand to hand high over the surf, and his father was presented with the welcoming symbols of hot baked pig and a large bowl of yams.

In their new home "my dear John," wrote Mary Williams of her husband, "made lime and plastered the floors. In a few days the principal chief of the island sent each of us nine pigs, with a roll of their native cloth, and all kinds of their fruit. I wish you could taste some of our bread fruit and arrow-root cakes. There are plenty of fowls here—sometimes we have fresh pork, and occasionally we kill a sucking pig, and get it cooked as well as you can in England who have large kitchen fires. Our method is to run a long stick through it, and to let the end rest on two forked sticks, and, having kindled a fire behind, a native sits to turn and baste it until it is well done. I only wish we had a cow and I should then be able to make some butter, but we get plenty of milk for our tea as we have five goats."

Huahine gave Williams a chance to learn the language, but its garden loveliness and the kindness of its people did not hold him. He had his eye on Raiatea, the largest of the islands, except Tahiti, and almost in the centre of the group. Its spacious reef, deep-water lagoon, its circumference of nearly fifty miles, and its peaks two thousand feet high gave Raiatea a majesty which appealed to Williams's imagination.

One day there landed on the beach at Huahine a giant, six feet ten inches high, Tamatoa, the King of Raiatea—he, too, had heard the whisper which was going round the islands of the new men and the new religion. He still worshipped Oro, the god of war, to whom more human sacrifice had been given than on any other island of the group. But he had already given it up. He and his people were waiting for teachers. So the Williams's went down to the giant canoe and were paddled westward to the pointing peaks of Raiatea. Tamatoa was proud that, like his two neighbouring chiefs, he was now equipped with a missionary, these strange white beings who spoke of a God who could not be seen, who kept one day a week differently from the rest and who could read the book writings and write on the white page.

"Can we have that piece of ground in which to build a house?" he asked Tamatoa's queen.

"Look forward!" she replied, "look backward, look on this side and on that! Look all round: for it is all yours, and wherever you say, there it shall be."

That decided Williams to build a big Mission House. He sketched out a framework of wood sixty feet long and thirty feet wide, with wattle walls. Over the walls was spread a coarse concrete made from turning coral into lime and mixing it with wet sand. There were three front rooms and four at the back, a French window and Venetian blinds. He planted a front garden overlooking the lagoon, and at the back had a poultry run of turkeys and chickens, and behind that a kitchen garden. At his carpenter's bench and lathe Williams worked in the open making tables and chairs for the new house. He was particular, too, about learning the language. He learned it by regular talks with the islanders. His quick, imitative mind picked up the sounds and as he worked at a window frame he kept an ear open to the gossip of the men plaiting thatch for the roof.

The large sitting-room of the Williams's—the wonder of the island—was filled every evening with native men and women handling the new-made chairs and sitting on the carpet which Mary Williams had brought all the way from London. One Saturday evening, when they had decided to keep out the people in order to have a little quiet, ten people managed to make excuses and come in. One of them was a rough naked man who had not been much in contact with the missionaries. He watched Williams for some time and listened to him reading from the Bible. Through the open window came the far-off roar of the surf on the reef and the music of the evening wind in the palms.

"Williams," at last he said, using the native name for Williams, "Williamu".

"Yes," said the missionary.

"When I go into the bush to pray, what should I pray? My prayer is: 'O Jehovah, give me Thy word in my heart—all Thy word, and cover it up there that it may not be forgotten.' "

A tear glistened in the eye of the young missionary. No one spoke.

"Williamu" believed that the Gospel truly had come to Raiatea.

Situated within the spacious lagoon of Raiatea was the island of Tahaa, six miles from the shore. To reach Tahaa Williams built a new boat sixteen feet long which could be managed by a couple of men. Plank by plank it was put together on the beach and the ribs were lashed in with native cord. No nails were used as Williams was anxious to show that native methods and materials could be adapted to larger boats. The boat sailed to Tahaa without leaking and the joyous people determined to build their own boats in the new fashion. To encourage them the three missionaries promised to give fifty nails each to the men who first started to build. An old chief soon had his keel laid, and his boat was the first exhibit of the island's *Society for the Encouragement of Arts and Sciences,* "which," wrote Williams, "we have established in our little way". A true touch of the progressive nineteenth century!

So the beaches and shores of pleasant Raiatea soon bore marks of the new way of life. The bushes and rocks along the shore were tidied up, and instead of two dirty native villages there was "a range of houses extending nearly two miles along the sea-beach in which reside about a thousand of the natives". The custom of families living and sleeping together in one large room was gradually changed and Williams reports on twenty houses with separate rooms for eating and sleeping.

A storm-driven canoe gave him once more the vision "beyond the reef".

One morning he saw from an island hill-top a small canoe sweep into the lagoon. The men in it were paddling wearily and he watched it come up to the shore. Out jumped a tall man and pushed the canoe up the beach. Williams ran to the beach and welcomed the strangers.

"Who are you?" he asked. "What is your island?" The canoe men eyed Williams fearfully, but when the people began to gather round with smiles and food the stranger's story began to come out.

"I come from Rurutu," he said, pointing southward. Williams later discovered that the island was three hundred and fifty miles away.

"Our gods have been angry, and the people have died of sickness. My name is Auura, a chief amongst them. Two of us fled from the island gods until their anger should go and crossed Tubuai. There we had food and set out again across the ocean. The great deep began to swell under the wind, and the storm came on us. The other canoe was swamped in the waves and the men drowned. But we were driven on for more days than can be counted on the hands with no food and water.

"At last we came to the island, Maurua, and there when we had food and drink we told our story, we told them of the gods on Rurutu and of the great sickness.

"The people of Maurua said: 'We, too, worshipped the gods and thought that evil came from spirits. But now we have had white men who have come with the story of the one true God and we all worship Him. We have no more killings and sacrifices, our wooden gods are destroyed and our temples burned down!'

"I wondered greatly at this," said Auura, "and asked them where I could meet the white men and get their religion. They pointed to the peaks of Borabora and Raiatea and we were driven to the entrance of your lagoon."

Auura and his men were led up the beach, and fed and housed. Their astonishment at finding the white men increased when they saw the rows of white cottages, neat gardens, tables, chairs, sugar-mill and the great house of God. They joined in the island life of going to school, learning to read, and regular worship.

As he listened to their story Williams heard the

surf on another shore and saw a chance of these men being missionaries to their own island.

They stayed for three months learning to read words and sentences in the Gospels and questions and answers from a catechism.

"I wish to go back to my people," said Auura one day to Williams, "to tell them of God and His Son, Jesus Christ." But while making ready for the long canoe journey a sailing ship came into the lagoon homeward bound for England. She was carrying a cargo of coco-nut oil as a gift to the Missionary Society.

Williams asked the captain to take the Rurutu men home. But when it was all arranged the chief looked worried. "How can I go to my land of darkness without a light in my hand?" he asked. "Send someone with me."

Williams called for volunteers for Rurutu in an assembly of the people. Two men stepped forward to go with the strange chief. Their people gave them presents for the other islanders—a razor, a knife, a roll of cloth, a pair of scissors, and in neat bundles they carried the Gospels in Tahitian.

As Williams watched them row across the lagoon to the homeward-bound ship he knew that for him as well as for them a new day had begun. Raiatea could no longer be his only island. The wide hemisphere of islands was open and needed an apostle.

22

One of the home-made boats had been hoisted aboard the ship in which the Raiateans were to return with news from Rurutu. They came back three months later paddling strongly through the entrance in the reef and into the lagoon.

For three hundred and fifty miles across the open Pacific they brought the good news from Rurutu. The home-coming chief had been rapturously received and the new religion established. The gods had been dethroned and a great church built with a pulpit made of the spears of war. There in the bottom of the open boat lay the evidence of Christian victory. The great wooden god Aa of Rurutu was brought to Raiatea and laid at the feet of the young missionary. It was hoisted above the heads of the people and they marched to the church for a Thanksgiving Service. Opening a little door in the back of the image Williams looked and saw a heap of small carved images in the hollow chamber. Aa was a master god but his reign was over.

The victory on Rurutu set Williams thinking. Without a visit from a white missionary the Gospel had taken root on Rurutu. The men from Raiatea had done it—why should not the Pacific be won by her own people? He walked up and down the coral beach on Raiatea with this thought in his mind. It would mean choosing the right men and inspiring them to go. But how were they to go? A passing ship might carry some and his home-made boats might sail a thousand miles. But they would not last in the stormy Pacific. From the beach he gazed across the lagoon to the breakers roaring on the reef. Their white foam glistened in the sun and the wide ocean beyond stretched away limitlessly to the Pole. There was only one way to win this great kingdom of islands. He must have a ship.

"We want a fine schooner," he wrote home to London, "of about twenty or twenty-five tons. If you would send one out it would be of great advantage and I suppose it would not be very expensive. It should be considered the Society's property and for the use of the whole of the missionaries. I have been attending to navigation for the purpose of teaching the natives."

That was Williams's first mention of a missionary ship, and from that moment he began his plan for a vessel. The "fine schooner" was his constant dream. By letter and conversation he made the dream a sustained truth which had to be accepted. A ship he would have whether it came from the Society in London or from his own hands on some Pacific beach.

3

OH! FOR A SHIP

IN AUGUST, 1821, John and Mary Williams went to Sydney for a short holiday.

But through all these days of holiday Williams knew that his chief aim in Sydney was to get a ship. He visited the quay side, interviewed captains and owners and kept his eyes open for a likely craft. He knew that there was little hope of the rapid extension of the Gospel amongst the islands unless the mission had command of a ship.

To back his impetuousness and his determination he was able to find, from a legacy left him by his mother, sufficient resources to buy a ship, and he was soon the owner of the new schooner *Endeavour*, a vessel of ninety tons. She was to be a trading ship as well as a Gospel ship, paying her way carrying cargoes, sugar and fruit from the islands to Australia and placing out native missionaries on her voyages.

In her, Williams and Mary and their son proudly set out across the Pacific on their return voyage to the islands, carrying in the new ship several cows, calves, sheep, and two bells for the new chapel.

The *Endeavour* sailed on to Raiatea. But Williams could not resist turning the ship south to Rurutu to see for himself what the native teachers were doing and to set his foot on another island. The first sight that met his eyes was a large plastered and pewed church on the model of the one on Raiatea. The whole island flocked to the building and Williams spoke to them from the text: "Blessed are your eyes for they see." "Neat, clean and respectable," are his comments on this island congregation. The women in bonnets and the men in hats. It was all an exact replica of his beloved Raiatea, and the native teachers had been busy about coco-nut oil and arrow-root. From the deck of the *Endeavour* there was lowered a large package containing five hundred catechisms and five hundred spelling books, and on the shore there was a wild scramble for the magic books. Williams had also written out in Tahitian the stories of two of his favourite Old Testament characters, Joseph and Daniel, and a Scripture catechism as well to supplement the meagre literature on Rurutu.

And so back to Raiatea and a rapturous welcome from the islanders; home to a "good house, plenty of ground, an abundant supply of the productions of the island, cows, ducks, geese, turkeys, pigeons and fowls"; home to a smiling happy community with a king and queen leading their people in public worship; home to the range of "plastered and whitewashed cottages and their own schooner lying at anchor near them." It was the "schooner lying at anchor" which delighted Williams most of all as he looked out at the familiar green heights sweeping down to the lagoon, and listened to the lazy wash of the blue waters on the coral beach. By fruit planting and sugar boiling the Raiateans soon had a stock sufficient to pay for the *Endeavour*.

By November 13, 1822, Williams reported that the *Endeavour* was ready for sea with a cargo big enough to pay all her expenses.

The *Endeavour* sailed for Aitutaki.

From her deck Williams, master at last of a ship, watched the peaks of Raiatea fade into the distance and the ship sailed into the south-west. For five days the endless rim of the ocean encircled the ship, and, sitting on deck in the cool shade of the thatched awning, Williams wrote down some instructions for his native missionaries. "Pay good regard to your own hearts," he writes. "Men will watch you to find little crooked places in your conduct. If you are of different opinions, let one give in. Do not be in haste to propose laws. Children are not fed with harsh food. A lazy missionary is both an ugly and senseless thing. We will not cast you off."

Words like these had inspired the native missionaries Papeiha and Vahapata for their twelve months on Aitutaki, and as the *Endeavour* drew near to the island Williams eagerly scanned the shore for sign of them.

A swarm of canoes shot across the lagoon as the ship nosed her way through the entrance. Swinging their paddles in the air the men cried: "The good word has taken root in Aitutaki. Good is the Word of God. It is well with Aitutaki. Look at the flag."

Looking towards the shore Williams saw two neat whitewashed cottages and by them a tall flagstaff at which was flying a white flag.

"The idols have been destroyed. Not one remains. The white flag is our sign."

Papeiha and Vahapata came on board and bit by bit, in excited and broken words, told the story of the Gospel's conquest.

"War came as soon as we landed," said Papeiha. "All the people on the island started to fight and we were dedicated to the gods of war. All our clothes and all our belongings were stolen."

"How did you begin preaching?" asked Williams.

"We did it by walking round the island and

28

speaking to the people. One day an old priest was explaining to the people that the god, Te-erui, made Aitutaki. We asked him who Te-erui's father was and where he came from. He did not know, so we began to speak about the Eternal God and some shouted, 'Surely this is the truth.'

"Other men," went on Papeiha, "plotted to kill us, and then one day the daughter of a chief fell ill. All the gods of the island were called on to restore her. But she died. Her father ordered all the gods to be burned.

"We stood in the grove of chestnut trees and gathered all the people together and spoke to them of the true God. Many of them brought their idols to be burned.

"We said to the people, 'Give us your idols and we will send them by ship to Raiatea. Then let us burn the *maraes* (temples) and then build a house for the true God.'

"It was done, Williamu, it was done! Then we burnt coral limestone and made whitewash and coral plaster. As the people saw us they thought we were roasting stone to eat. But with the coral plaster we took wet sand, and on the wattle of the church we cleared a space and plastered the wattle. Early next morning we took down the protecting cover and showed the beautiful white plaster.

" 'Wonderful, wonderful,' the people shouted.

'They can make stones, these men of the true God'." Williams sailed on to Rarotonga.

Searching for Rarotonga Williams came to Mangaia which Captain Cook had discovered forty-five years before.

Those on board the *Endeavour* saw the friendly white flag waving on the shore, so Papeiha led a canoe through the surf. There he displayed a few knives and oyster shells which enticed a few men out to the ship. But only one man ascended the ladder to the deck. From him Williams learned that the *Endeavour* was the first ship to call since Captain Cook, and as he looked round the deck at Williams and at the teachers who were preparing to land "every muscle in his Herculean frame appeared in motion". This shiver of fright sent him darting to his canoe and before Papeiha could entice him to stop he was pulling for the shore.

As there was no opening in the Mangaia reef, through which the ship's boat could go, Papeiha offered to swim ashore. The boat pulled in to the foaming breakers and from the stern Papeiha dived into them and was carried to the beach. This daring landing won the hearts of the islanders who promised to accept two teachers and their wives. But when the teachers landed the spears again came out and the bewildered visitors were hustled into the bush. One carried a saw which a Mangaian at once broke into three pieces and tied them about himself as ornaments. A box of bonnets, intended for the chief's wives was trailed through the water; the teachers' bedsteads were separated post by post and seized as a prize, and one chief, seeing two pigs for the first time, dressed them in his cloth and treated them as gods. Williams sorrowfully describes his teachers: "Their hats and bonnets had been torn from their heads, they had been dragged through water and through mud, and their shirts and gowns were hanging in ribbons about them."

Papeiha told the chief what he thought of this and he weepingly expressed his sorrow: "All heads are of an equal height on Mangaia!" He had no authority to protect his visitors. The gallant Papeiha himself, as the teachers scrambled for the boat was seized and nearly strangled by a *tiputa*— a long piece of cloth which was wound tightly round his head and neck.

So ended the first attempt to bring the Gospel to Mangaia. When the next attempt succeeded, it was pioneered by two young men, Davida and Tiere, from the tiny island church of Tahaa, near Raiatea. They, like Papeiha, swam ashore with New Testaments carefully wrapped in parcels on their heads.

Leaving the disappointments and dangers of Mangaia, Williams steered the *Endeavour* northwards to Atiu. Two native teachers had already settled on the island but Williams found them stripped naked and entirely dispirited by the opposition. His method in difficulties was to go to the chief.

"We had not been long near the island," he wrote, "when we perceived a large double canoe approaching us in the centre of which, on an elevated stage, was seated the principal chief. He was tall and slender and his aspect commanding. He was clothed in a white shirt having a piece of Indian print girt about his loins; his long and beautiful black hair hung gracefully over his shoulders and waved in the passing breeze as, with the motion of his body, he kept time to the rowers. We gave him a hearty welcome on board."

On board Williams had a chief from Aitutaki who took his brother from Atiu in hand and told him of the wonders of his island—the large white home of "roasted stone", and the burnt idols. The chief was led into the hold of the *Endeavour* and saw the grinning faces of some of the Aitutaki gods lying like so many baulks of old timber. He listened to Williams, as in the Sunday service the missionary read some powerful pieces from Isaiah and the Psalms about idols:

"They have mouths, but they speak not;
Eyes have they, but they see not;
They have ears, but they hear not:
Neither is there any breath in their mouths."

"Give me an axe," he cried after an all-night sitting with his Aitutaki friend, "give me an axe." He was out to destroy his gods.

But Williams had a bigger task for him than that. He persuaded Romatane to stay on board and act as pilot amongst the islands. Standing on the deck of the *Endeavour* he shouted to the men in the state canoe that he was going to Mitiaro and Mauke.

"Wait quietly at home until I come again. Be not sorrowful. Do not cut and scratch your faces and your bodies with the sharp stones and shark's teeth."

It was a strange mission for Romatane. Only a few years earlier he ravaged the islands with war, throwing bodies into the cannibal ovens, massacring children, and using living men and women, instead of tree-stumps, as rollers on which to launch his war canoes.

The chief of Mitiaro could hardly believe his ears when from the bow of the *Endeavour* Romatane shouted orders to burn the idols. Mitiaro was and is, only a coral bank fifty feet above the roll of the Pacific, two miles wide and three miles long;

but as its bewildered chief went back to his village he took with him Williams's greatest gift, a teacher, dropped over the side of the rolling ship. "Treat him kindly and listen to what he says," shouted Romatane. "I will come again, but not to the feast and dancing but to the building of the house of the true God."

Sixty miles to the southward this evangelistic mission of cannibal king and missionary came to Mauke with no reef and no lagoon and the gentle sweep of its coral banks melting into the great ocean. Coming on board, the islanders were astonished to see their king in the company of "white man" whom they tested by turning up Williams's sleeve and smelling his white skin.

As the ship's boat was launched a great cry went up: "It will upset, it will upset, it has no outrigger!" On seeing the goats they shouted out to those on shore: "Come and see the wonderful birds with great teeth upon their heads." Again a faithful teacher was put ashore and the *Endeavour* slewed out to sea seeking for the tracks to Rarotonga.

"And where is Rarotonga, Romatane?" said Williams as, in the bow of the *Endeavour*, the two men looked toward the horizon where Atiu lay.

"Over there, a day and a night's sail from Atiu."

A little later Williams asked the same question: "Where is Rarotonga?"

This time the chief pointed in an entirely different direction. Williams had been searching for the elusive island for weeks for he felt that this island would be the base of his future operations.

Remembering that the island king knew nothing of compass direction, but sailed his canoe by the position of land-marks, he asked him to shout when the land-marks were set on the track of Rarotonga. Williams watched the compass. Slowly the schooner sailed on for Atiu.

"Now," shouted Romatane. At Atiu the *Endeavour* took on board two castaway Rarotongans who volunteered to guide Williams home to their island.

"South-west by west" Williams's captain kept the course. But winds, and heavy swell between the islands constantly drove the schooner now east and now west. Day after day passed and the food began to run out. All day the two Rarotongans stayed at the mast-head anxiously watching for the first tip of their island peaks. But only the open ocean stared them in the face—its shining blue surface unbroken by ship or land. Only on the south-western horizon large grey clouds rolled up in gigantic formation. The captain's patience was exhausted. If they sailed on starvation and disaster awaited them. If they sailed back they might again find succour on Atiu.

Williams knew that this was true. But he also knew that Rarotonga must be there beyond the horizon where the great grey clouds were piled. They probably marked the whereabouts of the undiscovered island.

It was seven in the morning after a long night of patient watching and hoping that the captain told Williams the search must end.

"One hour more," he begged. "If, by that time, the island is not sighted we will turn back."

For the last time he sent the two Rarotongans aloft. Their keen eyes swept the misty horizon but no cry of "Land ho!" came from their lips.

They came down and mutely watched Williams pacing the deck.

"Up again," he cried. Four times they scaled the mast.

The last time was within a few minutes of the hour.

"Once more," urged Williams. "We can't be far off."

The morning sun was scattering the assembled clouds as the men went up the mast for the last time. The horizon lay clear and dazzling in the morning light and there, lying like a jewel on the blue bosom of the ocean, was Rarotonga.

"Land ho! It is the land we have been seeking."

Williams's eyes glistened and the schooner sailed

36

nearer the beautiful island mountain with its peaks green and pointed, with its deep valleys hung with vine and at their base the unbroken line of creamy surf breaking over the barrier of coral. It was Friday, July 25, 1823.

The *Endeavour* was carrying a canoe on board. Lowering it, Papeiha and one of the Rarotongans paddled for the beach. They were led up to Makea, the Rarotongan king, standing six feet high with his body beautifully tattooed and so coloured that his skin shone a bright orange.

Papeiha made his report and gave news of the true religion which all the islands were adopting.

"And is Williamu on board the ship?" asked Makea.

"He is," said Papeiha. "And your cousin Tapairu who has come back from Atiu."

"Let us go to the ship," said Makea.

The state canoe was launched and Makea boarded the *Endeavour*. After he had rubbed noses with Tapairu he said to Williams: "Are you the Kookees?"

"The Kookees?"

"Yes, we have heard from Tahiti of Captain Cook, and the white men that they brought sharp things which would cut down trees more swiftly than stone axes. No longer, we hear, do they use the bone of a man's leg and arm for tools for making canoes; nor do the children scream and cry while they have their hair cut as they did when it was cut with shark's teeth—for the Kookees have brought sharp, bright things that make it pleasant to have the hair cut."

That night the *Endeavour* stood off the reef for safe anchorage and Papeiha and the teachers with their wives slept ashore. In the middle of the night a man crept from the bush and seized one of the women.

"Let her be my wife," he urged to the half-awake group.

"She shall be the chief amongst all my wives."

Papeiha and the teachers fought hard to guard the women and at last the man retreated into the bush.

It was the sign that the conquest of Rarotonga would not be easy. In the morning Williams counselled caution. But Papeiha was determined to stay. Here was an island to win and a people to serve. Taking his New Testament and a few reading primers, he dropped into the canoe and, with strong strokes, drove it over the rolling waves till it broke through the summit of a breaker and swooped clean to the shore. He was immediately surrounded by a yelling crowd of islanders who waved clubs and spears at this daring apostle of the sea.

The *Endeavour* turned eastwards, with Williams

in the bow glad at heart. New islands had been won and new trophies added to the story of God's love for these islanders. Behind him he had again left the devoted Papeiha isolated and in danger.

As the schooner rolled homewards to Raiatea he remembered him in silence before God. It was a sad homecoming for the *Endeavour* too, which was sailed to Australia and sold to cover her costs. Once again Williams was without a ship.

4

MASTER OF A SHIP

IT WAS four years before Williams saw Rarotonga again. They were four tedious years in
which he chafed and complained at the slowness of
the plan to visit the islands. Raiatea flourished, but
that was not enough.

"It is our duty to visit surrounding islands," he
wrote home to London. "You have fourteen to
fifteen missionaries in these islands, missionaries
enough to convert all the islands of the South Seas,
and every one of these within a thousand miles of
us ought *now* to be under instruction."

His chance to sail westwards again came in
1827, when the ship *Haweis* was chartered to take
new missionaries, the Pitmans, to settle on Rarotonga. With the eight-months-old Samuel in his
mother's arms, the party landed in a high sea. The
landing was nearly disastrous. In the act of handing
over the child the boat, with Williams standing in
the gunwale, was caught on a high wave and dashed
against the side of the *Haweis*. Tugging at his frock
coat Mrs. Pitman pulled him back into the boat,

with the child in his arms, while Mrs. Williams sat terror-stricken "in the bottom of the boat with her face covered". The news spread round the island that "Williamu" had come, and Papeiha led a great crowd down to the beach to welcome him. The shining face of the native pioneer told Williams its own story.

"What happened, Papeiha, after I left you?" he asked.

"Oh! Williamu, I was taken up to the house of the old chief Makea. A big crowd followed me. One cried: 'I'll have his hat,' and another: 'I'll have his shirt,' but I was saved by the chief, who said: 'Speak to us, O man, that we may know the business on which you are come.'

"I told them, Williamu, the story of the one true God, of the burning of the idols of wood and cloth, but they all cried out: 'What! burn the gods! What gods shall we then have, and what shall we do without the gods?'

"We began family worship amongst ourselves, Williamu, and a few came to look on, and another chief sent for me and asked me to stay by him and pray. I prayed, Williamu, but he dropped off to sleep. Then I went to a great festival where the people were painted in stripes of many colours, with caps made of shells and birds' feathers. I carried my Testament with me and they began to

41

say: 'That's his god, what a strange god, he carries it about with him.'

"Then a priest came and said he would burn his idol and also gave us his little boy to teach. Then the chief, Tinomana, sent for us to go to his home in the mountains. He said he wanted to be a Christian and to burn his idols. They brought four great idols to our feet, Williamu, and I took off their clothing and made a fire. As the flames roared up the people danced in fury and called us 'drift-wood from the sea, two rotten sticks driven on shore by the waves'. But the idols have gone, Williamu, and we teach the first-born of every chief in our school."

As Williams listened to the miraculous tale of Papeiha he was already planning a new House of God which, in seven weeks, was finished by the people themselves. It was while working on the chapel one day that Williams wished to send a message to his wife to send down his square. Taking up a thin chip of wood he wrote the message on it in charcoal and asked a chief to go with it to Mrs. Williams.

"What must I say?" the chief asked.

"Nothing," replied Williams, "the chip speaks for itself."

The chief, who had lost an eye in battle, looked at Williams sorrowfully.

"How can it speak? Has it a mouth?"

"Go and see," replied Williams.

The chief watched Mrs. Williams look at the chip, go to the tool chest and bring out the square.

"For Williamu," she pointed.

"But I did not hear the chip speak," he said.

"Oh, I did," laughed Mrs. Williams. The chief leaped from the house and ran shouting through the village, holding the square in one hand and the chip in the other.

"See," he shouted, "Williamu can make a chip talk."

As the mystery of writing on the wood slowly dawned on him he hung the chip round his neck and proudly strutted amongst his friends with this marvellous charm.

Papeiha amused the missionaries at night with the tale of Tom, one of the teacher's cats, who in his first few days on Rarotonga, was regarded as a monster from the deep. On one of his peregrinations he visited the house of a priest who had destroyed his idol. His howls and scratchings on the open doorway awoke the man and his wife. But all they could see was two large round fires glowing in the darkness of the doorway.

"Get up and pray," urged the priest's wife.

The priest began in terror to shout his newly learnt alphabet as a prayer! Tom bolted, and the

43

priest and his wife slept again, convinced permanently of the efficacy of prayer.

On another occasion Tom visited the old temple of the gods and found a warm, comfortable spot for his sleep. While he was there a group of men came secretly to offer gifts to the spirit of the old gods. They saw Tom and hesitated. He mewed at them. The leading man rushed back in fear, shouting to his companions: "Here's a monster from the deep, here's a monster from the deep." The party fled and later returned with blackened faces and bodies, and equipped with spears, slings and war caps. Tom gave one wild look at them and sprang for the open door, scattering his enemies. Alas! poor Tom met his death by creeping later into a house, and venturing to sleep under the same cloth as a fearless warrior who roused his household, shut the door and despatched the cat with clubs and spears.

But still Williams had no ship to call his own.

As the modern steamship enters Avarua Bay in Rarotonga there is a little cove to be seen from the deck with a gentle slope down to the sea. In this secluded spot in the autumn of 1827 Williams built his own ship, his final solution to the problem of having no ship at his command. A home-made ship of seventy to eighty tons fit to sail the Pacific had long been in his mind and the enforced stay on Rarotonga gave him his chance.

Marshalling his books on mechanics, his tool chest, the willing labour of the chiefs and the people, and his own commonsense and flair for mechanical contrivances, Williams began his ship building.

His first need was a pair of bellows for his forge. There was no leather on Rarotonga except that which might be got from the skins of four goats. One was giving a little milk, so the other three were sacrificed. The skins were cured and roughly tanned, and after four days' work Williams managed to produce a working pair of bellows. Then came the rats of Rarotonga, and overnight ate up the stretched goat-skins, leaving Williams with the bare frame of the bellows! But a bellows was vital if the few pieces of iron on the island were to be forged for the ship. So Williams invented a box-bellows, twenty inches square and four feet high. There was a valve at the bottom and a damper similar to the piston in the cylinder of a steam engine. This was loaded with stones to force it down and a long handle attached on which ten men pressed and let go suddenly. It forced out a tremendous blast, but also sucked back the flames of the forge so that at the first trial it was ablaze! A small valve hole soon put this right, and to keep up a succession of blasts a second bellows was clamped to the first, and another ten men laboured to blast air into the forge. The contraption worked!

The precious bits of iron were beaten out on a stone anvil into pins and clamps for the beams of the ship. But the supply was very limited, and a large number of hard wood pins were shaped and driven in through holes made by hot iron. As he had no saw with him Williams split trees in half with wedges, and his helpers adzed them down with small hatchets. There was no steam available for bending wood, so when a shaped piece was needed the people searched the wood for crooked trees and split them in half.

The keel was laid down, sixty feet in length, of hard aito, or iron-wood, and the breadth designed to be eighteen feet. Plank by plank her ungainly sides were clamped and nailed together, and the seams stuffed with coco-nut bark, dried banana stumps and native cloth. Ropes were made from the bark of the hibiscus tree, and when the masts went up the best sails were found to be those mats the Rarotongans slept on. They were quilted to add resistance to the wind.

Unpainted, and with poor comfort for crew and passengers, this ship of faith was edged gently into the sea in November, 1827, and aptly christened the *Messenger of Peace*. At its mast was hoisted a flag with a dove flying on a blue ground with an olive twig in its mouth. A flag as suitable for

Noah's Ark as for Williams's *Messenger*! Once floating, the difficult question of the rudder had to be settled. There was no piece of iron on Rarotonga large enough for its pintles, so a pickaxe, a cooper's adze and a large hoe were made to serve. The *Messenger* answered to the helm and Williams proudly walked her rough deck while his friend Chief Makea devoted himself to the home-made pumps which kept the bilges free.

The ship was a triumph of ingenuity and faith, and Williams was eager to test her seaworthiness.

Heaving the box of stones, which acted as an anchor, on deck, he put to sea. Outside the reef one of the crew let the foresail go in the wind and brought the mainmast crashing to the deck. Struggling with wind and tide, Williams brought the ship safely back and, after repairs, set out for Aitutaki. It was a courageous voyage across one hundred and forty miles of open ocean and back again. The most nervous person on board was Chief Makea who, in his bunk, groaned at the crashing of the seas on the ship's timbers, and followed Williams about on deck as he took the sights and kept the ship's course. From Aitutaki they brought back a cargo of pigs and cats. Cats were wanted on Rarotonga to keep down the plague of rats which ran over the tables at meal-time, nestled in the beds and disturbed family prayers by their screeching. These lively rats even ate a leather trunk belonging to Mrs. Pitman, and during one night devoured her only pair of good shoes.

Having proved herself equal to a local voyage the *Messenger of Peace* was prepared for the long voyage eastwards to Tahiti, and then to Raiatea, before Williams carried out his intention of going westwards to Samoa. Flapping her way into Papeete harbour during the night the *Messenger* was taken for a pirate ship, but the island was reassured after they saw the honest broadcloth and smiling face of Williams come ashore.

Williams was now master of a ship, and his vision ranged beyond Rarotonga to Samoa and the wild New Hebrides.

Eastwards he knew the islands and the seas well, but westwards was a new world almost uncharted and unknown. The creaking sails of the *Messenger* bent to the steady winds, and Williams kept his hand at the helm, and watched the home-made rudder, now held by well-made pintles, cleave the waves as the ship rose to the swell.

5

SAILOR TO SAMOA

"SEE how the ship rides. Tomorrow we should see the tops of the Samoan mountains," cried Williams in his excitement.

The cloud-capped heights of Savaii came in sight the next day. The ship was sixty miles out at sea but the bold, forest-covered sides of the mountains rose clearly from the wide base of the sea. Williams's heart quickened. This was the largest group of islands to which he had brought the Gospel.

Running to the leeward of the island the *Messenger* was soon surrounded by canoes. It was the Sabbath day and the *Messenger* dropped anchor in a great bay. The quilted sails of the *Messenger* flapped in rags about the masts, and in the strong current of the straits the anchor dragged and the weary crew had to fight hard to get back to shore. On Tuesday morning they reached the settlement of Sapapalii from where a message was sent to King Malietoa.

At four o'clock in a heavy shower of rain, Malietoa boarded the *Messenger*, and thus began the long

49   D

connection of the London Missionary Society with the royal house of Samoa. "He was," says Williams, "about sixty-five years of age, stout, active, and of commanding aspect. He was immediately invited into the cabin; and, having no clothing except the girdle of *ti* leaves, worn by the people generally, and it being excessively cold and wet, we gave him a large piece of Tahitian cloth, in which he wrapped himself, and with which he appeared much pleased. We then stated our object to him, and he said he had heard of the *lotu* and, being desirous of instruction, was truly glad we had come to impart it. . . . We then made him a present of two strings of large blue beads, an axe, a chisel, a knife, and some Tahitian cloth."

The happy beginning was nearly ruined by a tragedy. On the deck of the *Messenger* was a small brass blunderbuss which, unknown to Williams, had been loaded with eight bullets and put back in its usual place. Malietoa began innocently to prod the musket and look down its muzzle. He cocked it and pointed it towards Williams and was about to snap the trigger when someone artlessly suggested: "Perhaps it's loaded!" Unperturbed, Malietoa climbed over the side of his canoe, and through the sea-mist, was paddled ashore proudly wearing his piece of Tahitian cloth and fingering his two strings of blue beads.

"*E vaa lotu*—the praying ship has come," ran the word through Samoa, and the island prepared for the landing.

But when the morning dawned the *Messenger* had drifted out to sea and almost out of sight of land. The ship's boat was lowered and Williams and Barff, the other missionary, in shirt sleeves began to row. It was nine in the morning and the shore seemed only a few miles distant across the calm water. But the sun was setting by the time the two weary men, by rowing and bailing, drew near. Malietoa saw them struggling with the leaking boat and took them off in a fast canoe.

Evening light was already falling over the island and the forests threw gloomy shadows to the water's edge. Along the shore an excited crowd of Samoans had come to welcome "the man of the Word", carrying torches of dry coco-nut. A great beacon threw its flares into the night sky near Malietoa's house and, as the two tired men came out of the canoe, a passage was forced through the crowd by men armed with clubs who smote the head of any man or woman who blocked the way. The glare of torchlight fell on the two men in wide black hats, broadcloth and kerchiefs, weary in legs and arms after the long day in the boat. Complaining of this, Williams and Barff were seized bodily and hoisted at full length on the uplifted arms and hands and so brought triumphantly, if not gracefully, to the royal hut of Malietoa where he was sitting in the light of the torches.

Eight teachers were left in the islands under the care of Malietoa and his brother, who each received "one red and white shirt, six yards of English print, three axes, three hatchets, a few strings of sky blue beads, some knives, two or three pairs of scissors, a few small looking-glasses, hammers, chisels, gimlets, fish hooks and some nails." The return for these riches was fifteen pigs and a large supply of vegetables for the *Messenger* as she made ready to sail.

"Come again, Williamu, come again," shouted the canoe men as the *Messenger* flung her foresail to the wind and drew southwards across the broadening sea.

There are few episodes more remarkable in seafaring history than the voyages of this amateur ship under an amateur sailor in one of the most dangerous oceans. Williams's own native boldness, and a touch of cocksure composure, accounted for much of his success. But he was not foolhardy in the handling of his ship. On some voyages he hired a captain—usually a young man from a passing whaler—and no doubt felt complimented that the home-made ship responded to the professional touch. The *Messenger* was even sent down to New

South Wales on one voyage to take a missionary and his wife. What the waterside men of Sydney, used to the stately Australian clippers, thought of her is not recorded. But the ship did her job and her name stands worthy of salute as on a last long voyage Williams turned her once more to Samoa.

The *Messenger of Peace* came once more into the beautiful strait between the Samoan islands, and Williams and Malietoa met again.

The fine old chief had by this time, with all his household, wives and young men, become Christians.

Between the two visits serious trouble had occurred between Malietoa and the chief of Manono Island. Some twenty years before, this chief had killed Malietoa's favourite daughter after taking her prisoner. His sons had constantly urged revenge and now there was a chance. But the old man proved faithful to the little he knew of the new religion. "It is," he said, "a religion of peace. I must live and die under it." Taking Malietoa with him to Manono, Williams brought the two chiefs together in friendship and wrote down the words they said to him: "We two have now but one heart."

With his teachers well established and happy in the care of friendly chiefs, Williams turned again southwards while the women of Malietoa's court chanted a farewell chorus:

The birds are crying for Williamu
His ship has sailed another way.
The birds are crying for Williamu
Long time he is in coming;
Will he ever come again?
Will he ever come again?

It was the last voyage of the *Messenger* to Samoa. The work of the home-made ship was done. Coming back to Rarotonga, Williams sent her to Tahiti to be sold while he made plans to go home to England.

6

SEAMAN TO THE END

FOR four years John Williams went up and down Britain telling the story of the South Seas on his ships. His hope was to collect enough money to buy a new ship which he could sail from London to Samoa.

At last in April 1838 his dream came true and he stood proudly on the deck of the *Camden* outward bound for his beloved parish of the sea, and in November 1838 his ship dropped anchor in the spacious harbour of Pago Pago in Samoa.

Williams was home again. Across the broad bay he saw the thin screen of waving palms and heard the wash of the breakers on the shore. A warm wind from the island brought the familiar smells of the bush, and as the *Camden* rode at anchor the canoes began to shoot out from the beach.

"It is Williamu, it is Williamu," shouted the canoe men. "He has come back, he is in the ship of religion."

The news spread round the islands and Williams entered again as a victor into the kingdom he had won.

Four young men came off in a canoe to welcome him. They were finely built young Samoans and out of respect to Williams they were wearing hats. Climbing up the side of the *Camden* they stood in simplicity before him and slowly lifted their hats. Together they said in Samoan, while holding their hats rather awkwardly:

"Good indeed are God's arrangements. He has heard our prayers and brought you back at last."

Williams smiled and thanked them.

Good indeed were God's arrangements. For his eye caught the central mast of the *Camden* from which fluttered the purple flag of peace with the white dove carrying the olive branch of everlasting promise. His dream had come true. He had a new ship, and he must sail on.

To sail on meant penetrating into the islands of the New Hebrides, an almost unknown group lying due west from Samoa. The tiny isles were on Williams's maps only faint dots on the ocean. They were the natural gateway to the innumerable groups which lay scattered through the Coral Sea leading on to the great island of New Guinea. It was to visit this immense parish of islands that Williams had brought out the *Camden*, and almost immediately on arrival in Samoa he began laying his plans.

Williams could not rest in Samoa any more than

he could be content with routine missionary work on any other island.

His mind was always towards the west where the *Camden* might sail unvisited seas.

The last few months of Williams's life which began with an eastward voyage to Rarotonga were overshadowed by a sense of impending happenings. One of his colleagues, Barnden, was drowned while bathing and Williams saw the event as casting some shadow across his own future. He remarked after the funeral: "I, perhaps, shall be the next." The plan to go to the New Hebrides was opposed, too, by Mrs. Williams who was frightened by the tales of the islanders' fierceness. But there is no sign that Williams allowed any of these omens to change his plans, and meanwhile the *Camden* enjoyed a royal progress through the eastern seas.

At Rarotonga the great event was the landing of the five thousand copies of the New Testament in Rarotongan, which the islanders eagerly bought.

Then happened one of those amusing but annoying incidents which Williams always enjoyed.

Preparing to leave for Tahiti all the baggage of the party was sent on board the *Camden*. The plan was to sail the next day. But next morning there was no *Camden*. The wind had so increased, and with it the swing of the current towards the shore, that the captain had been compelled to stand out to sea and the ship had disappeared beyond the horizon. A day passed and there was no sign of the ship. From the top of the Rarotongan hills telescopes were sighted towards the four corners of the horizon, but no ship was seen. A week passed and the stranded party wanted changes of clothes. Some of them were easily provided for, but Williams was an outsize which no coat or shirt on the island would fit. So he organized a tailor's shop and out of a dungaree material fitted himself with temporary suits until the ship reappeared. As the week lengthened into a fortnight the party began to fear the ship had been lost, and Williams went down to the cove where he built the *Messenger of Peace* and discussed plans to build another ship. But on the tenth day the *Camden* reappeared, having been saved from disaster by the captain's seamanship, and she carried Williams and his colleagues on to Tahiti.

This last visit to the islands of his first home in the South Seas was a mixed experience.

It was a brilliant moonlit scene as the *Camden* came to little Huahine. The sea was a dead calm and the silent groves of the palm trees threw long shadows on the water while into the harbour floated the tall sails of the *Camden*. She was towed by two rowing boats and only the regular beat of their oars broke through the still night. He opened a new chapel on the island which stood at the margin of a small lake in the midst of a thick plantation of trees formerly sacred to the gods. On Raiatea—so dear to him by many ties—he was alternately depressed and encouraged. The island was less neat and tidy than when he left it but this, he felt, might have been due to the building of thirty large decked boats on which every islander had been busy. Houses were neglected and gardens disordered, but he heard of wild young chiefs coming to the mission house and sitting among the rocks and learning their letters as their fathers did before them. Williams was reluctant to leave Raiatea. He walked the familiar shore and looked again on the lagoon which for so long had cramped his vigour, and from the rise of the foothills he saw the wide ocean which had beckoned him to explore its distances. His last word to "beloved Raiatea" was that he would come again, and his last salute to the island was from the deck of the *Camden* as he watched the top of the green-crowned hills fade into the horizon.

It was April 26, 1839, when the *Camden* again sighted the Samoan Islands.

There were many discussions in the Williams's household about the voyage to the New Hebrides. Mrs. Williams was still against it because of the dangers which were known to be very real in the Hebrides, and also on the grounds that so much work remained to be done in Samoa. But no arguments of danger or prudence could prevent Williams from obeying the call which he heard from the untouched shores. Besides, the ship he had prayed and worked for was now his, and there was already a good band of workers on Samoa.

"Don't land on Erromanga, John," was the continual plea of Mrs. Williams in the last days before the *Camden* sailed. She had heard dark tales about the island, and the sight of the *Camden* ready to sail filled her with fear.

"Don't land on Erromanga, John!"

The echo of his wife's voice floated round him as the *Camden* weighed anchor and stood out to sea. The twelve Samoans, huddled pathetically together on the deck, watched the receding island, while Williams and his two colleagues, Harris and Cunningham, stood behind them, each silent with his own thoughts.

It was November 4, 1839.

Putting into Apia the next day a blind man came to Williams in the mission house.

"Teacher Williams," he said, "I am a blind man, but I have a great desire to go with you to the dark lands. Perhaps my being blind will make them pity me, and not kill me, and whilst I can talk to them, and tell them about Jesus, my boy (putting his hand on the head of his son) can read and write and so we can teach these things."

It was the benediction which Williams needed. The word of the blind man followed him as the *Camden* slipped through Samoan waters to the "dark lands" of the west.

On Saturday, November 16, they were near Fotuna, the first of the New Hebrides islands. Williams noted the perpendicular cliffs reaching to the sea, and the complexion of the men who came out to meet them, "not black like that of the negro, neither brown like that of the other South Sea islanders, but of a sooty colour. Their faces were thickly smeared with a red pigment, and a long white feather was stuck in the back of their heads." One chief was enticed on board and was dressed up in a red shirt and a piece of cloth, in which he strutted about the deck; but the swaying of the ship brought on sea-sickness and the proud man was willing to lie down and cry: "I'm helpless, I'm dead."

The morning of November 20, 1839, dawned very brightly with the *Camden* slowly sailing past the southern shore of Erromanga watching for canoes from the shore. Williams was elated by the reception on the first two islands. He knew the reputation of the islanders, and of their savage treatment of other European visitors, especially sandalwood traders, and he had hopes of a friendly reception on Erromanga.

In the landing on Erromanga Williams seems to have gone in the first boat himself contrary to his usual practice of sending native teachers ashore first. Perhaps this display of four Europeans in a boat with four sailors frightened the Erromangans and stirred them to attack. The landing at first was friendly and Williams walked up the beach to the bush. What happened on the beach at Erromanga is best read in the calm observant words of Captain Morgan who went ashore with Williams:

"We pulled up the bay, and some of the natives on shore ran along the rocks after the boat. On reaching the head of the bay, we saw several natives standing at a distance; we made signs to them to come toward us, but they made signs for us to go away. We threw them some beads on shore, which they eagerly picked up, and came a little closer, and received from us some fish-hooks and beads, and a small looking-glass. On coming to a beautiful valley between the mountains, having a small run of water, we wished to ascertain if it was fresh, and we gave the chief a boat-bucket to fetch us some, and in about half an hour he returned running with the water, which, I think, gave Mr. Williams and myself more confidence in the natives. They ran and brought us some coco-nuts, but were stilll extremely shy.

"Mr. Williams drank of the water the native brought, and I held his hat to screen from the sun. He seemed pleased with the natives, and attributed their shyness to the ill-treatment they must have received from foreigners visiting the island on some former occasion.

"Mr. Williams remarked, he saw a number of native boys playing, and thought it a good sign, as implying that the natives had no bad intentions: I said I thought so too, but I would rather see some women also; because when the natives resolve on mischief they send the women out of the way; there were no women on the beach.

"At last he got up, went forward in the boat, and landed. He presented his hand to the natives, which they were unwilling to take; he then called to me to land some cloth out of the boat, and he sat down and divided it among them, endeavouring to win their confidence.

"I stopped to see the boat anchored safely, and then walked up the beach towards the spot where the others had proceeded; but before I had gone a hundred yards, the boat's crew called out to me to run to the boat. I looked round, and saw Mr. Williams running straight for the sea, with one native close behind him.

"I got into the boat, and by this time two natives were close behind me, though I did not see them at the moment. By this time Mr. Williams had got to the water, but, the beach being stony and steep, he fell backward, and the native struck him, and very soon another came up and pierced several arrows into his body.

"As soon as I got into the boat, I headed the boat towards Mr. Williams, in hopes of rendering him some assistance, but the natives shot an arrow at us, which went under the arm of one of our seamen, through the lining of the boat into a timber, and there stuck fast. They also hove stones at the same time.

"The boat's crew called out to me to lay the boat off; I did so and we got clear of the arrows. I thought I might be able to get the body, for it lay on the beach a long time. At last I pulled alongside the brig, and made all sail, perceiving with the glass that the natives had left the body on the beach. I also ordered a gun to be fired, loaded with powder only, thinking to frighten the natives, so that I might get the body; the natives, however, made their appearance, and dragged the body out of sight."

"Williamu is dead."

The news spread round the islands by canoe and messenger and to the lonely Mrs. Williams in

Samoa it brought confirmation of her worst fears.

"Alas, Williamu, alas, our father."

Samoa's grief was deep and tearful and hundreds came to weep with Mrs. Williams.

From Australia H.M.S. *Favourite* went up to Erromanga and very reverently the crew collected the bleached bones of Williams on the shore and carried them to Samoa. As the ship approached the island the first canoe was guided by a middle-aged man.

"Alas, Williamu," he shouted across the sea and then, as if overcome with grief, he dropped his paddle into the canoe, bent his head and wept. The *Favourite* drew to the shore past hundreds of bowed heads and in silence the casket of bones was carried ashore.

They rest today in a church at Apia just underneath the hill on which Robert Louis Stevenson sleeps—the two apostles to Samoa of friendship and peace.

7

SHIPS OF THE LINE

"WILLIAMU is dead."

It was a mournful *Camden* which four years after the tragedies on the beach at Erromanga came up the English Channel. She had gone out in the full glory of Williams's adventure which had stirred Britain, and now in 1843 her sails in London Pool drooped in sorrow.

"Williamu is dead." Even the *Camden* herself was declared unfit for further voyages in the treacherous Pacific. The need for a ship was again urgent.

Then someone, who has not been recorded, made one of those inspired suggestions which immediately change the faces of people and problems.

"Why not," he said, "ask the boys and girls of the churches to build a ship of their own and call it *John Williams?*"

At that moment the spirit of the great missionary lived again. John Williams is not dead! He sails on!

All up and down the country children began collecting small sums to build *John Williams I*. Two mill-girls gave fifteen shillings by selling their dinner-hour loaf and going hungry. Pit-boys worked all night for a shilling and gave it. A little boy offered his bright new half-crown, and a girl sold her favourite doll for four shillings. Farthings and sovereigns added glory to the children's new ship.

Down at Harwich a ship was building which looked a likely vessel. She was purchased out of the £6,000 which the children raised, and on March 20, 1844, was launched with the name *John Williams*. She was a barque of 296 tons, 105 feet long with a breadth of 24 feet 8 inches and depth of 16 feet. In June 1844, she dropped proudly down the Thames on a glorious morning with a pennant flying bearing her name, and in the November of that year she was amongst the islands.

Her welcome there was rapturous. "He has come again. Williamu is here."

The people of Rarotonga and Samoa realized the deep meaning of the gesture in naming the ship after their apostle. For two months the ship sailed amongst the Samoan islands and while she was there the Samoan children collected native produce to the value of £400 as their contribution to the work of the ship. In the tracks of Williams the ship sailed amongst the wild New Hebrides looking for an opportunity to land teachers on Erromanga. Then after three years she turned home to

Britain in 1847 with coco-nut oil and arrow-root as gifts to the Society in London, which sold for nearly £2,000.

Five months later she again began the long trek to the Pacific loaded with 5,000 Tahitian Bibles, 4,000 copies of the *Pilgrim's Progress* and, amongst other cargo, an iron chapel, printing machinery, and iron tanks in which the people might put their oil contributions.

Tales of treachery still came from the Hebrides. One teacher was visited by a party of thirty savages who had come to kill but professed to be friends. For a day and a night they waited and at last entered when the teacher and his family were at prayer. Their hatchets trembled in their hands and their arms refused to strike. Courageously the teacher ordered them to depart and very meekly the men walked out. Coming home to their own district they were laughed at for not being able to kill men who were merely teachers!

"The *lotu* must be a great thing," they replied, "and must be true, for we who have been accustomed to kill men could not kill the teachers. Our arms were heavy, and they trembled, and we could not strike."

Sixty men set off in their canoes to prove the truth of this tale, and determined to kill the teachers. But half-way on their journey a storm arose and drove them on to the rocks. Surely the *lotu* was powerful.

The *John Williams* gathered a harvest of stories and deeds which she brought home for the second time to Britain in 1850 and for the third time in 1855. These visits brought the South Seas very near to Britain—much nearer than in these days of easy communications. By going down to the West India Docks and aboard the *John Williams* you could smell the great ocean, and see the palms and sandy beaches. Weeds of the sea still clung to her sides and on her deck were the great cargoes of arrow-root and oil as offerings from the island people. Thousands of boys and girls went down in horse omnibuses and ran up the little gangway to board their own ship. The South Seas and all their romantic far-away tales became true as they trod the clean scoured decks and saw the crew preparing for the next voyage.

In 1850 the children raised £3,200 to repair her thoroughly, but two years later on the reefs of the island of Borabora she was nearly wrecked. The strong force of the current drew her towards the reef, and for six hours the crew rowed hard to prevent her going finally on to the rocks. As a last resort the captain threw overboard his water casks, ballast and firewood, and as the tide rose the men pulled the ship off the rocks.

On the last day of June 1860, the *John Williams* reached London once more, and again the children raised over £5,000 for her repairs and outfit. In this voyage she penetrated to the remote islands of the Northern Cook group—Manihiki and Raka-hanga and visited tiny Puka-puka, or Danger Island, which today is reached very rarely by a missionary. Puka-puka is nearly all lagoon with three main villages set triangularly on the reef. As the ship lay-to for the night the captain noticed a drift of the current towards the reef, and he at once had out his whale-boat and the crew pulled the ship out to sea. A friendly breeze helped and the danger seemed to be passed. But the wind dropped and the shoreward drift set in again. At four in the morning they were close to a reef, and the long unimpeded rollers were thrusting the ship to the sharp coral edge. Heavily the ship struck stern foremost. But the great receding wave carried her off only to be met by a greater incoming one which crashed the ship higher on to the reef. At five o'clock as the dawn came up, a boat was launched and the forty passengers and crew taken off while the pounding process of the ship against the coral went on. Every time she struck the ship's bell rang loudly, and before midday the *John Williams*, battered in bow and stern, slipped off the coral reef into deep water and sank out of sight.

The islanders had watched the ship as soon as she struck but feared to go near her, believing that she was a slave ship kidnapping young men and women for the silver mines of Peru.

Thus passed *John Williams I*.

The great name and the great commission were transferred to *John Williams II*, in 1866. She was built in Aberdeen and for her the children raised £11,000. From the first she ran into gales and storms. On her way out to the Pacific a terrific gale smashed her rigging in the Channel and she was compelled to shelter in Portland Roads. It was boisterous weather all the way to Australia, but the children's ship stood up bravely to the wind and sea. Leaving Australia she made for the New Hebrides where the old trouble of a shoreward drift nearly wrecked her. On the reef at Aneitium she stuck for a day and a night with the water pouring in through a leak. The islanders dived underneath, as she lay caught on the grounding coral, and stuffed blankets soaked in tar into the hole and nailed them in tightly. By pulling in boats and by lightening the cargo she was got off and went down to Sydney for repairs.

On January 8, 1867, she called at Niué, where there is no safe anchorage and no sheltered harbour. She "lay-off" in the ocean some two and a half miles out. It seemed safe enough and far away from the breakers, but the dreaded shoreward drift set in. Three boats were let down and fourteen men strained at their oars—but still the terrible current carried the ship nearer to the rocks. Swinging broadside to the shore the ship began tossing amongst the breakers, and the men in the boats gave up their hopeless task. Wave after wave lifted her three hundred tons on to the sharp fingers of the rocks, and the beautiful ship, the pride of so many thousands of children, began to smash to pieces in the glare of the torches which the Niuean people brought down to the shore.

Her destruction brought dismay to Britain and Australia, but fortunately her cost was almost fully covered by insurance and within two years *John Williams III* from the same Aberdeen shipyard was launched, a graceful, speedy barque of 186 tons with the legend "Peace on Earth" painted on the starboard bow, and on the port bow "Goodwill to Men". She was spared the long journeys between Britain and the Pacific by making her home in Sydney and for twenty-eight years she sailed in and out past Sydney Heads without damage or loss of any kind. Not once was there a claim on the insurance company and the fine barque weathered all the gales of the Pacific and seemed instinctively to avoid the dreaded shoreward currents of so many islands.

She was the pioneer to New Guinea in 1874 when she sailed into Port Moresby harbour with the pioneer missionary, W. G. Lawes, on board, and for twenty-one years she thrashed her way through foaming seas and threaded the deceptive Coral Sea from Samoa to Papua carrying teachers and their wives to the new stations along the seven hundred miles of the Papuan coast. John Williams's name was carried farther than he had dared hope for—all through the Eastern and Western Pacific the purple flag with the dove of peace became familiar in harbours and coves and the name of the pioneer was known through his ship. He sailed on in her, the last sailing ship to fly the L.M.S. flag. When she was sold in 1895 for £600 to a Sydney trader she vanished on her first voyage.

The old ship which had weathered a hundred tight corners in the Pacific was never heard of again, as if she had made up her own mind that she could not sail under any other flag.

The time had come for steam.

So *John Williams IV* was built on the Clyde and launched in 1893. The children again set to work and raised over £17,000 for this steamer which could also be a three-masted schooner. Again her home was in Sydney and her voyages to the islands and Papua took place three times a year, covering some 30,000 miles a year.

She was the real ocean tramp of the South Pacific, known in all the ports from Sydney to Suva, and from Port Moresby to Pago Pago. Beachcombers, scallywags, retired "blackbirders", exiled traders, government officials, consuls and merchants knew the mission ship with its poky funnel, deck loaded with coco-nuts, laughing boys and girls, and the purple flag of peace at the masthead. She pioneered before the days of the modern steamship lines running out from New Zealand and Australia. She was home and friends, letters and papers, provision stores and shops to isolated missionaries on a hundred islands. Her smoke off the reef meant furlough and home, new heart and fresh courage, visits to friends and opportunity to plant the Word in fresh places. The *John Williams IV* was loved over the wide Pacific.

Being able to steam meant that she kept a pretty regular time-table, and nearly every island planned its life and events by the appearance of the ship. She was part of the established facts of life for many lonely places. She meant school for boys and girls, coco-nuts in time of famine, news of the outside world and comfort to the small congregation of God's people. As well as Samoa and Papua she went north to the Gilbert and Ellice Islands, and crossed the Equator to those isolated atolls set in an immense hemisphere of water. Without her the lines of communication would be broken and the precious links of the Gospel snap. By the time her day in the Pacific was over she had sailed a million miles and her last voyage was done in 1929.

She was sold to a trader on the China coast and one day a missionary standing on a Shanghai wharf thought he saw a familiar look about a ship tied up at the quay-side. Looking carefully at the flaking paint on her bows he could see beneath the thin coating the bold lettering *John Williams*. He lifted his hat in salute to the old ship.

Was another ship necessary?

A lot of people asked that question when the *John Williams IV* was making her last voyage. Coasting steamers now visit the coast of Papua, and sail amongst the Cook Islands. Samoa is on a direct route of Pacific liners and now the air lines come there too. It looked as if missionaries and supplies might be able to get to most of the islands without a special ship to carry them. But those who argued so, forgot the lonely scattered islands of the Gilbert and Ellice group which lie away from trading and liner routes. There a Christian community of 15,000 as well as 120 native pastors and six British missionaries need the service of a ship. There are the outposts of Nauru and Ocean Island, the valuable phosphate islands, and all this great parish to be visited and administered properly needs a ship.

So *John Williams V* was launched at Grangemouth in 1930 and for her the children of Great Britain, Australia, New Zealand and the South Seas raised £18,000. Officially she was described as a three masted fore-and-aft schooner with auxiliary motor power, with a registered tonnage of 226 tons. Her home was moved from Sydney to Suva in the Fiji Islands and from there she set out three times a year on her voyages round the island.

She swung northward from Suva to Funafuti at a speed of five knots. Then on to the Gilberts— Beru, Onotoa, Tabiteuea, Tarawa and the rest. The names stand in the typewritten analysis of her voyage as romantic scraps of her far-away kingdom. Her three slender masts peeped above the reefs and the low-lying atolls. She was not able to use her sails as much as her captain wished—only fourteen and a half hours on one voyage. The little diesel engine chugged away down below eating up its four gallons of oil per hour and requiring another four gallons a day for lubrication. Oil is expensive and the captain longed for a good run with the sails. But the ship kept to her time-table as much as possible as the routine of the mission life depended on her. One of her most important duties was to take boys and girls to school at the large school of Rongorongo, on the island of Beru. She collected them from their island homes and delivered them at the school every six months.

Can you imagine little Ariati on Tabiteuea, one of the Gilberts? He is nearly fourteen. His father has promised him that he shall go to the big school at Rongorongo on Beru. There must be four hundred coco-nuts, boxes of dried fish, and sixty bottles of coco-nut treacle for fees and food. He must have a mosquito net, camphor-wood clothes box, Bible, hymn book, hurricane lamp and an alarm clock. His sister has given him an embroidered pillow case, and his father five pounds to be cared for by the school.

Ariati's dream comes true.

With his packages and boxes and forty bundles of coco-nuts he is rowed across the lagoon. Outside the reef the *John Williams* waits. On the deck is the captain with a group of shouting boys in the white singlets and blue and gold badge of Rongorongo School. Ariati scrambles up the gangway and the crew hoist up his baggage. The engine-room telegraph clangs and the ship sails from Tabiteuea with the frantically waving handkerchiefs fading on the inner shore.

John Williams V was school omnibus, postman, newsboy, milkman, grocer and carrier of the Word in these wide blue-green seas beneath the Southern Cross.

Here is a scrap from the deck log book of *John Williams V* signed and sealed by the Master and Chief Officer:

Saturday

6.00 a.m.	Crew washed decks.
8.00 a.m.	Fine and clear.
8.52 a.m.	Let go line.
8.54 a.m.	Full speed.
9.10 a.m.	Cleared (away to Funafuti).
9.55 a.m.	Clock back 42 minutes. Fine and cloudy weather.
4.00 p.m.	Light breeze. Confused sea.

Sunday

4.00 a.m.	Light wind and slight sea. Fine.
6.00 a.m.	Crew washed deck.
9.00 a.m.	Clock back five minutes.
10.00 a.m.	Sabbath Day observed.
1.00 p.m.	Crew at rest.
8.00 p.m.	Rain squall.

Monday

Crew painting gangways.

Tuesday

Crew cleaning brasswork.

Thursday
  Discharging cargo.

Saturday
  4.00 p.m.   Mission party boarded.
  6.00 p.m.   Cleared lagoon (away to Nui).

The song of the fifth *John Williams*, written by
Joyce Reason, celebrated the story of the ship as
she sailed:

Taut and trim in Suva Bay, decks new scrubbed
  and brasses gleaming,
White and bright as spindrift spray, lies *John
  Williams* dreaming!
Now the hurricanes are past, now the stormy
  season's done,
You may spread your sails at last, time your
  voyage was begun!

> Oh, John Williams,
> Our John Williams,
> Let your engines run!

"Empty holds and decks all bare, how can I go
  winging
To those far-off islands, where they look for
  what I'm bringing?
Samoa, and the Ellice Isles, Funafuti, Vitapu,

Wouldn't welcome me with smiles; Abaiang,
    Makin, Beru,

        Cry, 'John Williams,
        Our John Williams,
        We depend on you!' "

Packet out of Sydney town, steaming north to
    far Fiji,
Lets her gangway ladder down, dumps her bales
    on Suva quay:
"These for you, John Williams; Look! Papers,
    pens, and type for press,
Coloured cloth for binding books, likewise some
    for schoolgirls' dress.

        Ho, John Williams!
        So, John Williams!
        More to come, I guess!

A liner come from London brought me bags and
    bags of Britain's mail.
Letters full of loving thought, and packages of
    goods as well,
And New Zealand and Australia, they kept
    adding to my freight,
Loaded me and bade me sail her, pass to you the
    welcome weight.

80

Hey, John Williams!
'Way, John Williams!
Off, or you'll be late!"

Now the snowy sails unfurled northward bear
    our gallant ship,
Goods from all across the world now begin their
    final trip,
League on league of tossing sea! Like a white
    sea-bird she flies
Dipping, rising gallantly, till against the pearly
    skies,

> Our John Williams,
> Brave John Williams,
> Sees the islands rise.

Sees the danger line of spray on the jagged
    barrier breaking.
Anchor down and boats away, for the narrow
    inlet making!
What a shout along the shore, echoing up the
    coral sands!
"Ho! John Williams comes once more!" Run-
    ning feet and waving hands

> Meet John Williams,
> Greet John Williams,
> Come from far-off lands.

In and out among the isles, up and down the
    Southern Seas,
Stormy miles and sunny miles, sullen calm or
    spanking breeze,
Bearing pastors to their flocks, boys and girls
    to school again—
God keep safe from reef and rock, gust and gale
    and hurricane
        Our John Williams!
        Grant John Williams
        Never sails in vain!

All your many errands done, southward bound
    for Suva's port,
Eyes you've brightened, hearts you've won, with
    the welcome gifts you brought,
Say, of all you leave of lift, at your many ports of
    call,
Was there one most valued gift, one most
    precious thing of all?
        Well, John Williams,
        Tell, John Williams!
        Something great or small?

"One more cherished thing I took than all gold
    was ever minted—
Just a little sober book, plainly bound and
    closely printed.

82

Yet upon those leaves is writ earth and heaven's
  most wondrous story:
God our Father speaks through it; here is seen
  the Saviour's glory.

> I, John Williams,
> Your John Williams,
> Bear the Word of God."

The end of this well-loved little ship came at
Christmas 1948 when she was blown on to a reef
off the Samoan Islands. For a long time her mast
could be seen above the breakers still bravely
pointing upwards. She had sailed and served well
for eighteen years.

8

MORE SHIPS OF THE LINE

WAS a new ship really necessary? That question was again asked when the service of *John Williams V* came to an end in 1948.

Much had happened amongst the Pacific Islands during war-time to break down the isolation of their lives. The great Pacific airliners between the United States and Australia and New Zealand gave new links to the islands, and there were new inter-island ships to carry goods as well as passengers.

But the churches of the islands still needed the kind of intimate service which only a ship like the *John Williams* could give. So the call went out for a new ship, and the children of Britain, Australia and New Zealand, as well as the islands themselves, responded nobly to the amount of over £30,000, and *John Williams VI* came into the line of the famous ships.

She was a quite new addition to the *John Williams* line—a motor vessel, oil-driven and equipped with all the latest aids of navigation. A sturdy, coastal trading ship of 400 tons when she was bought, *John Williams VI* was adapted for her new job in a British shipyard, and was given her new name by a British princess—Princess Margaret.

The idea of inviting Princess Margaret to name the new ship brought a fresh glow of romance to the *John Williams* line. The Princess responded very happily to the invitation and at the Tower Pier in London she spoke from the ship to a crowd of children about the "children's ship of goodwill". It was a new and appropriate name for the *John Williams*, this stalwart and well seasoned vessel which left the Thames in November 1948, and after sailing halfway round the world came to the Gilbert and Ellice Islands and then to her new home at Suva in the Fiji Islands.

From Suva *John Williams VI* sailed regularly to the islands for fourteen years. She also voyaged to faraway Papua to carry Samoan pastors to other mission stations; to the Cook Islands for the church assemblies; to Samoa to show the flag of peace was friendship once again.

But her main task was in the Gilbert and Ellice Islands, those coral atolls of the Pacific which only a ship can reach. One long trip across the sea brought her to Nauru and Ocean Islands—almost a separate cluster of islands in the Gilberts.

Until the beginning of the century no one valued

these islands as being anything more than two ordinary coral islands which grew rather good coco-nut palms.

Then one day in 1899 a man stumbled across a piece of rock which was propping open the door of a Sydney office. He chipped off a piece of the rock, ground it up, tested it and noticed its strong phosphoric acid reaction.

He asked where it came from. He was told Nauru in the Central Pacific. An expedition was quickly organized to the island to see whether there was any more rock like this on the island, and on a May morning in 1900 the prospectors sighted Nauru. They sank holes all over it and discovered that the island's crust was composed entirely of a rich deposit of phosphate. So was its neighbour, Ocean Island.

The two islands now are amongst the richest in the world. Phosphate is needed by the world's farmers, gardeners and cultivators. Fertiliser manufacturers need it for their super-phosphates. Upon the right amount of phosphate in the soil depends a good yield of milk, butter, cheese, meat, wool, hides and tallow. An eight-thousand-ton cargo of phosphate from Nauru makes fourteen thousand tons of super-phosphate, enough to treat a hundred thousand acres of dairy farm, or 400,000 acres of wheat-growing lands.

So out of the village calm of the Gilberts the *John Williams* anchors off Ocean Island which is equipped with all the latest devices of a great industry's plant. The island rises sharply to a mountain peak from the floor of the sea. Two hundred and sixty fathoms down gigantic buoys are anchored to hold the anchors of twelve-thousand-ton ships as there are no natural moorings. Loading piers float out to meet the ships, carrying rails, engines and trains of trucks. About a thousand natives drawn from the islands work on the phosphate deposits, and are provided with houses, food, hospital attendance and forty shillings per month. Seven hundred Chinese labourers are also employed, and live in a special location with dwellings, mess-rooms, bathrooms, offices, and spacious recreation room. Probably no labourers in any part of the world have such good conditions of life and work.

The phosphate workers on Ocean Island love singing, and the Ellice islanders amongst them form a great male voice choir which often leads a "singing service", swelling into hymns and choruses like a great organ. Groups from various islands sitting on the floor of the church, sing hymns and anthems in eager competition. "They seemed to enjoy their Christianity," remarked a visitor. "I am sure we western folk can learn much in our

worship from the three South Seas 'S's'—
Simplicity, Spontaneity, Sincerity."

I

Nauru and Ocean Island were the westward
limits of the voyages of the *John Williams VI*.

From there she sailed southwards to the Ellice
Islands which have Funafuti as the port of entry
to their ocean parish. The nine Ellice islands divide
between them about four thousand people and half
a dozen Europeans.

Look them up on an ordinary map and you will
hardly find the dots which mark them, lying to the
north-west of Samoa. One of those dots is little
Nukulailai with its two hundred people.

Nukulailai was the first to hear about the Gospel
over a hundred years ago. It happened as a result
of a church assembly on Manihiki, in the Northern
Cook Islands, twelve hundred miles to the east, in
1861. The Rakahangan representatives were sailing
homeward to Rakahanga after the meeting, and
had almost reached their own beach when the wind
changed violently and the large double canoe with
its big mat sail and platform was swept backwards
into the open sea. All night they struggled to reach
Manihiki again, but when morning came there was
no blur of land on the horizon.

There were six men, two women and a child on

board, with four gourds of water and a small heap of coco-nuts. The men had to bale for life. Elikana, the deacon, kept up their courage and headed for Samoa or Rarotonga. The wind helped them and then swept them helplessly past islands they were unable to reach. They caught rain-water in the spread sails.

For seventeen days they drifted without course or plan. Six weeks passed and they drifted on, living on sharks' flesh and guarding with famished care the last six coco-nuts. It seemed useless to keep up the fight and the balers lagged in their ceaseless task. One volunteered to go on if the others would. The rest voted them the last six coco-nuts.

The eighth Sunday came with half a coco-nut left. On the broad bosom of the Pacific Elikana led the desolate men and women in worship for the last time. As the lovely evening drew on he saw a tiny blur on the horizon. They all watched it, and hope grew. The evil wind turned and drove them straight for the reef, and by midnight they were in the breakers which crashed them on to an islet of the atoll. Three perished and the rest staggered to the beach and lay down for dead.

Throughout all the perils of those eight weeks Elikana had kept his New Testament and hymn book dry. He wrapped them inside his scanty clothes, and the first thing he showed to the astonished Nukulailaians were these two supposedly magic books. It was this, so they argued, which had preserved him over the stormy ocean and brought him to their island, and as a symbol of the divinity of the books Elikana was compelled to divide them into pieces, giving a page to each household on the island. Then he began to teach the great simplicities of the Gospel that he knew, and at last the grateful islanders sent him to Samoa to learn more so that he might be their pastor.

Landing on one of these little coral atolls is an exciting adventure calling for skill on the part of the canoe men and always the possibility of a drenching for the missionary.

"We watch the skyline," writes a present-day missionary, "and presently we point excitedly to a tiny dot; the green top of a coco-nut palm has come into view. Then soon we see a row of palms making a dark line against the clear sky: then the white breakers can be distinguished at the edge of the coral reef, and later still the sandy shore.

"The ship slows down, the hum of the engines stops, the anchor is lowered; out from the shore come many tiny canoes. How fast the men ply their paddles, and how skilfully they guide their frail craft through the surging waves on the reef out to the ship. And we lean over the sides watching.

First the chief, who represents the government, must come on board, and then the rest follow—some up the gangway, and others swarming up the ropes which dangle from the cross beams.

"But we must pack our boxes and hurry down the rocking gangway into a canoe as it rises on the swelling waves, perch ourselves as securely as maybe on the piece of wood placed across the dugout, put our belongings on the out-rigger, and away towards the reef. How mountainous the waves seem, and how green! How cruel are the jagged rocks of pink and grey as the suction of the current leaves them bare for a moment.

"And there we wait watching the spray, until suddenly, with a shout, the men dip their paddles with all their strength, and we rise on the crest of a high wave, and as it curls over we slide safely into the smooth waters inside the reef. Sometimes a following wave breaks over our heads, swamping the canoe and throwing our luggage into the sea; but at last we are drawn safely to shore, where all the people of the village—men, women and children—are waiting to greet us.

"Slowly we make our way up the sloping coral sand, gleaming white in the blazing sunshine, smiling a greeting to the brown children who are dressed in grass skirts and strings of shells, shaking hands with the grown-ups, exchanging news with our old friends, until we reach the open house, thatched with palm leaves, which is to be our shelter for the day."

II

After her fourteen years in and out of Suva *John Williams VI* was proving an expensive little ship to run. She used a great deal of diesel oil and being based on Suva she always had a long run home from her essential job of visiting the Gilbert and Ellice Islands. So in 1960 a decision was made to build a new ship *John Williams VII* much smaller and specially designed for inter-island visitation.

About 125 tons as compared with *John Williams VI* 400 tons, the new ship was registered as a yacht, and how trim she looked at Tower Pier on November 29, 1962 when Princess Margaret came to name her. Her length is 85 feet, width 23 feet and her speed 9 knots. With a galvanized steel frame, she is built of teak wood and her hull has a special nylon protective sheathing. She has two diesel engines, radar short-wave radio, echo sounding and direction finding equipment, and she carries a motor life-boat and a whale-boat for shooting the reef.

With money from the sale of *John Williams VI* and with extra collections by the children the new ship was provided by spreading her cost over her years of service. Her sea parish is not so great as her predecessors' as she will live permanently at Tarawa in the Gilbert Islands, which is now the centre of island, church and school life.

The sixteen tiny atolls of the Gilberts make up only 166 square miles of land, while the nine islands of the Ellice Group have only fourteen square miles. Land is precious for growing coco-nuts and for harvesting the copra which is the main crop of the islands. But the sea is also part of the islanders' life—and a ship to visit these remote spots is as necessary as ever it was.

Although *John Williams VII*'s circuit of voyages is more confined than those of the previous ships she does strike out across the ocean every two years to the Cook Islands and every year to the Phoenix Islands.

The Phoenix Islands lie a thousand miles to the east of the Gilberts, a dozen small specks on the surface of the great ocean. Gilbertese people live on the islands and work in the big coco-nut plantations, and how expectant they are for the coming of the ship with its news of home and the friendly visit of the Gilbertese pastors and the missionary.

The ship's visits to the Cook Islands take her back to the area where the home-made ships of John Williams himself came from. It was on Rarotonga that he built his *Messenger of Peace* and

93

from there he sailed to Samoa. Like all the islands of the Pacific Rarotonga is being swept into the whirl of modern life in spite of being an island.

Here is what a missionary on Rarotonga says about life there:

The ordinary family working on its plot of land for subsistence and using that as its sole income is now uncommon. Most families have someone who gets paid a wage if not regularly then at least during the export season for fruit. Most families have members in New Zealand, most are planning to send other young folk there. The drift of active young people to New Zealand has increased and presents problems to all youth work and potentially to the economy of the islands. There is more money about, more sophistication and more freedom for young people. Traditions and conventions count for less and less initiative, education and business ability for more and more. Although the chiefs have a formal right of leadership I do not think their word carries very much weight. For a good many old people the Church is now about the only solid secure thing in the social framework—government changes its form and its mind so often, land tenure is beset with legal problems, the tribe is a dying force—but there is the

Church, the old original Church, beloved, cared for and respected.

Many young people of the islands criticize this old way of life which they often say is out of date and belongs to the past. They long to be away from the cramped conditions of island life and to sail beyond the horizon to new worlds. But they love the ship *John Williams VII*. She is a sign to them of the friendship and love of other people beyond the horizon and to see the ship's flag is to know of the world wide message of goodwill and peace.

As long as there are people and churches on these South Seas islands so a ship will be needed to visit them. John Williams sails on in his ships and the message of Christ is the same as he preached a hundred and fifty years ago.